HISTORY IN
DEPTH

THE POOR LAW

Susan J. Styles

Head of History, Settle High School, North Yorkshire

M
MACMILLAN
EDUCATION

First published 1984
Reprinted 1986, 1987

Published by
MACMILLAN EDUCATION LTD
Houndmills, Basingstoke, Hampshire RG21 2XS
and London
Companies and representatives
throughout the world

Printed in Great Britain by
R.J. Acford
Chichester

British Library Cataloguing in Publication Data
Styles, Susan J.
The Poor Law. — (History in depth)
1. Public welfare — England — History
2. Poor — England — History
I. Title   II. Series
362.5′8′0942   HV245
ISBN 0-333-36543-7

CONTENTS

Acknowledgements

The author and publishers wish to acknowledge the following photograph sources:

Bedfordshire County Council p 39 top; BBC Hulton Picture Library pp 11, 39 bottom, 41, 45, 52; British Library pp 49, 54; Courtesy Trustees British Museum p 30; Fotomas Index p 14 top; Herts Records Office pp 17, 19, 21; *Illustrated London News* Picture Library pp 7, 28, 29, 50; Mansell Collection pp 14 bottom, 26, 36, 37, 44, 46 top; Mary Evans Picture Library p 33; Metropolitan Bradford Libraries p 27; Public Records Office, London p 35 right; *Punch* pp 6, 10, 35 left; Staffordshire County Record Office, 47; West Yorkshire Archives Service, Bradford p 53; William Salt Library, Stafford, 46.

The publishers have made every effort to trace copyright holders, but where they have failed to do so they will be pleased to make the necessary arrangements at the first opportunity.

PREFACE

The study of history is exciting, whether in a good story well told, a mystery solved by the judicious unravelling of clues, or a study of the men, women and children whose fears and ambitions, successes and tragedies make up the collective memory of mankind.

This series aims to reveal this excitement to pupils through a set of topic books on important historical subjects from the Middle Ages to the present day. Each book contains four main elements: a narrative and descriptive text, lively and relevant illustrations, extracts of contemporary evidence, and questions for further thought and work. Involvement in these elements should provide an adventure which will bring the past to life in the imagination of the pupil.

Each book is also designed to develop the knowledge, skills and concepts so essential to a pupil's growth. It provides a wide, varying introduction to the evidence available on each topic. In handling this evidence, pupils will increase their understanding of basic historical concepts such as causation and change, as well as of more advanced ideas such as revolution and democracy. In addition, their use of basic study skills will be complemented by more sophisticated historical skills such as the detection of bias and the formulation of opinion.

The intended audience for the series is pupils of eleven to sixteen years; it is expected that the earlier topics will be introduced in the first three years of secondary school, while the nineteenth and twentieth century topics are directed towards first examinations.

1 PEOPLE AND POVERTY

When we talk about poverty today, we might be thinking of the sort of lives lived by people in some of the developing countries, such as Bangladesh or Brazil. When people in Britain use the word 'poverty' in connection with themselves, they might just mean that they do not have a car, or a colour television, or that they cannot afford a holiday that year. For the people of nineteenth century Britain, poverty meant something very like the poverty of the developing nations today.

mither: bother

> *You went down one step ... into the cellar in which a family of human beings lived. It was very dark inside. The window-panes were many of them broken and stuffed with rags, which was reason enough for the dusky light that pervaded the place even at mid-day.... They began to penetrate the thick darkness of the place, and to see three or four little children rolling on the damp, nay wet, brick floor, through which the stagnant, filthy moisture of the street oozed up; the fireplace was empty and black; the wife sat on her husband's chair, and cried in the dank loneliness.*
>
> *'See, missis, I'm back again. Hold your noise, children, and don't mither your mammy for bread, here's a chap as has got some for you.' In that dim light, which was darkness to strangers, they clustered round Barton, and tore from him the food he had brought with him. It was a large hunk of bread, but it had vanished in an instant.*
>
> Elizabeth Gaskell: *Mary Barton*, 1848

Can you imagine what it would be like to live like this? To have a damp, dark cellar as your home, and to be thankful for a hunk of bread brought to you by a sympathetic stranger? The people in this novel lived in Manchester, which was the centre of the cotton textile industry, but many factory workers living in other towns would have recognised only too well the dirt and the hunger, even if we, today, find it difficult to believe that people could have lived in such a way.

The family who lived in that cellar was only one of the great number of families who were very poor indeed. The adults in this family were unemployed, but poverty was something which did not only hit those without a job. There were thousands of working people, in town and country, who had jobs, but who earned such low wages that they found it difficult to feed and support themselves and their families. There were also large numbers of agricultural labourers who could only find work between spring and autumn; in the winter they were without a job and had no means of supporting themselves. Workers in the textile industry frequently suffered from unemployment when trade was slack. If the slack period lasted for months this might lead to the temporary closure of the mills, which could bring disaster to a whole town.

5

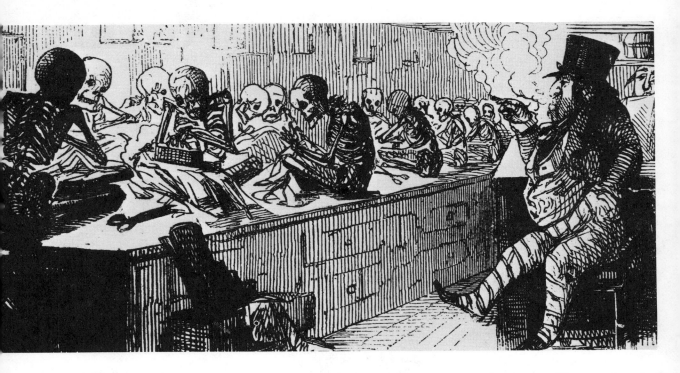

Cartoon from the magazine Punch, *published in 1845*

Look carefully at the cartoon. Obviously it is not telling us that the fat, prosperous and rather nasty-looking man on the right employed skeletons to sew clothes for him! The skeletons are only representing people, and they are saying to us that these people were so poor that they could not afford to feed themselves properly. We shall look later at what else the cartoonist is trying to say to us.

We have not, so far, looked at any sources about real people. Were real lives any different from the lives of the people in the novel and in the cartoon?

In many of the cottages ... the beds stood on the ground-floor which was damp three parts of the year; scarcely one had a fireplace in the bedroom, and one had a single small pane of glass stuck in the mud wall as its only window, with a large heap of wet and dirty potatoes in one corner. Persons living in such cottages are generally very poor, very dirty, and usually in rags, living almost wholly on bread and potatoes, scarcely ever tasting animal food, and consequently highly susceptible of disease and very unable to contend with it.

susceptible of: likely to get
contend: cope

Report by John Fox, Medical Officer of Cerne Poor Law Union,
Dorset, 1842

This extract describes how people lived in rural Dorset. The illustration on the next page tells us a similar story. These people were suffering from the same sort of grinding poverty which was described in the fictional sources. More evidence of poverty comes from the weekly shopping list of Elizabeth Whiting, a 40-year-old widow with four young children.

Poverty in rural Dorset in the mid-19th century

1 shilling (s.): 5p
2½ old pence (d.): 1p

Pays 3s. a week rent, owes £1 13s. Does charing and brushmaking; earned nothing this week; last week 3s.; the week before 5s. 8d.

Expenditure

Dec. 15, 1839.   s.   d.

Sunday: Bought on Saturday night, Potatoes 1½d., bacon 2d., candle ½d., tea and sugar 2d., soap 1½d., coals 2d., loaf 8½d.   1   6

Monday: Tea and sugar 2d.; butter 1½d.; candle ½d.;   4

Tuesday: Coals   2

Wednesday: Tea and sugar 2d.; candle ½d.; wood ½d.; potatoes 1d.   4

Thursday: Coals   1

Friday and Saturday   –   –

       2s. 5d.

S.R. Bosanquet: *The Rights of the Poor and Christian Almsgiving Vindicated*, 1841

We can imagine Elizabeth trying to keep her growing children fed, clothed and warm on a pitifully small wage. We can also, perhaps, imagine how Elizabeth herself might have gone without food in order to give more to her children.

The last three sources (the report, the weekly account and the picture of poverty in Dorset) are about real people. These people were not famous; they are known to us only because people like John Fox reported on their way of life to show how badly off the poor of the time were. The other sources are different. Elizabeth Gaskell was writing a novel, and the cartoon is from *Punch*, a magazine which has always criticised, in words and in cartoons, anything of which it disapproved. Are these sources less useful in helping you to understand poverty in the nineteenth century than the sources about real people? They do not give you facts and figures and true life stories. What do they tell you?

When you read Elizabeth Gaskell's novel you hear her crying out against the desperate plight of the poor; when you look at the drawing you see the cartoonist criticising the employers who paid starvation wages.

This is very important indeed, because our study of the past must involve more than just learning the facts. We must try to understand how people at that time felt about the problems which they had to face, even if they themselves were not poor. These sources help us to do this, and what we learn is that poverty was so bad that novelists wrote about it, cartoonists drew pictures about it, and official reports were put together about it. How did both the poor and those who had to find a way of looking after them, cope with the situation? We shall find this out in the following chapters.

Using the evidence

1   Look again at the extract from Mrs Gaskell's novel, the extract from John Fox's report and the picture of the Dorset family. Then give the evidence from these sources upon which you think the following statements could be based.
    (i) Poverty used to bring hunger and disease.
    (ii) The lives of the poor in rural areas were often no better than the lives of the poor in the industrial towns.
    (iii) Poverty and dirt were often found together.
    (iv) The homes of the poor lacked light and air.

2   Now read this extract from an official report:

    Cellar in York Street., a man, his wife, family altogether comprising seven persons: income £2 7s. 0d., or 6s. 8½d. per head; rent 2s. Here the family occupy two filthy damp unwholesome cellars.

    In a dwelling house, Store St., one sitting room, one kitchen and two bedrooms, rent 4s. per week, a poor widow, with a daughter, also a widow with ten children making together thirteen in family; income £1 6s. 0d. per week, averaging 2s. per head. Here there is every appearance of cleanliness and comfort.

    John Scott of Carr Bank, labourer. Wages 12s. per week; a

wife and one child aged 15; he is a drunken, disorderly fellow and very much in debt.

George Hall of Carr Bank, labourer. Wages 10s. per week; he had reared ten children: he is in comfortable circumstances.

George Locket of Kingsley (boatman), wages 10s. per week, with a wife and seven children: his family are in a miserable condition.

George Mosley of Kingsley (collier), wages 18s. per week: he has a wife and seven children: he is saving money.
Edwin Chadwick: *Report on the Sanitary Condition of the Labouring Population of Great Britain*, 1842

a) Use this extract, and the extracts from the novel and Fox's report, to explain whether you think that the statements given in Question 1 would have applied to all poor people in Britain in the nineteenth century.

b) All the families mentioned in Chadwick's report were poor, but they were not all living in misery and filth.

Using only this extract, suggest why some families were living in more comfortable circumstances than others.

3 This is part of a poem written by Thomas Hood in 1843. He wrote it after hearing about a poor widow with two children whose job was making trousers at 7d. (about 3p) per pair. She earned only seven shillings (35p) a week.

O men with sisters dear!
O men, with mothers and wives!
It is not linen you're wearing out,
But human creatures' lives!
Stitch—stitch—stitch
In poverty, hunger and dirt,
Sewing at once, with a double thread,
A shroud as well as a shirt.

shroud: a garment in which people were buried

When you have read the poem, look again at the *Punch* cartoon, then try to answer these questions.

a) What is the cartoonist trying to tell us?

b) Can you suggest any ways in which the poem backs up what the cartoon is telling us?

c) Thomas Hood wrote this poem to show how he felt about the life of the poor widow. Does this mean that the cartoonist based his cartoon on a real case? If not, why did he bother to draw the cartoon?

4 The following two sources show us, in different ways, what it was like to be poor. Source **A** is a list of the personal

belongings of a woman admitted to the poorhouse in Anstey, Hertfordshire:

A *An inventory of the goods of Eliz Brown Taken*
by the parrish officers Octobre ye 29th 1756
a Table a Square Table a Leather Trunk
a Cubbard a Looking Glass a poridge pot
a frying pan a pair of Tramells a pair of bellows
2 wheels 1 keel 1 pail a bed.

tramells: hooks from which pots were hung over the fire
keel: a container in which liquids used to be put to cool

B The Poor Man's Friend, *published in* Punch, 1845

Use these sources to help you to answer these questions:
a) How does each of the two sources show us what it was like to be poor?
b) Why do you think that the list and the drawing were made?
c) What are the differences between the two sources?
d) Which of the two do you think gives the more vivid impression of what it was like to be poor? Explain your answer clearly.

THE OLD POOR LAW

As long as there have been people living together in societies there have been those who have been less well off than others. This may have been the result of illness, old age or just inability to find a job, but the problem has always been the same: who should look after these people if they could not look after themselves?

It was in the sixteenth century that, for the first time, governments in England began to try to create a national system for dealing with the poor. Until then, the poor were very much the concern of individual villages and towns. One of the main sources of money for looking after the poor was the giving of alms – money or food given as an act of charity or kindness by richer people in the community. Alms-giving did not end when the Tudor governments of the sixteenth century started to involve themselves in looking after the poor; all people who saw themselves as good Christians would give money to those in need. Even today, when a good deal of money and help is given by the Welfare State in Britain, people still like to give money to organisations which provide help and relief for those who are less well off.

Look at this picture drawn by Abraham Bosse in the middle of the seventeenth century. It shows rich people giving food to beggars. They probably felt that God would look kindly upon them for giving alms in this way.

Offering Alms to the Poor *by Abraham Bosse (1602–76)*

1 How does the artist show us that the people on the right of the picture are poor?

2 Explain whether you think that the picture tells us more about
   a) the artist's view of poor relief in the seventeenth century, or
   b) the way in which the rich gave help to the poor in the seventeenth century.

3 The artist did not paint this picture from real life. Does this make it useless as evidence about seventeenth century poor relief?

Elizabeth I and the Poor Law

To begin the story of the poor and how they were cared for, we are going back to the time of Queen Elizabeth I, who reigned from 1558 to 1603. During her reign, Acts of Parliament were passed to encourage each parish to look after its own poor. By the end of Elizabeth's reign, there had been many different attempts by various towns and villages to solve the problem of poverty in their own area. Acts were passed to try to improve poor relief and to force people to give money to their parish authorities for looking after the poor. Everything was so complicated that, in the end, Elizabeth's government gathered all these Acts together into one.

Here is an extract from this Poor Law Act, which was passed in 1601:

vagabond: a wandering beggar
sturdy beggar: able-bodied beggar
apprehension: arrest

> . . . *every person which is by this present Act declared to be a rogue, vagabond or sturdy beggar, which shall be . . . taken begging, vagrant or misordering themselves . . . shall upon their apprehension . . . be stripped naked from the middle upwards and shall be openly whipped until his or her body be bloody, and shall be forthwith sent from parish to parish . . . the next straightway to the parish where he was born . . . and if the same be not known, then to the parish where he last dwelt . . . one whole year, there to put himself to labour as a true subject ought to do; or not being known where he was born or last dwelt, then to the parish through which he last passed without punishment. . . .*

Questions
1 What was supposed to happen to sturdy beggars and vagabonds when they were caught if a) it was known where they were born, and b) it was not known where they were born?

2 What does this extract from the Poor Law Act tell us about the government's attitude towards beggars and vagabonds?

3 Read the following statements:
   a) The first police force in England was formed in 1829.
   b) Few ordinary people travelled more than a few miles outside their own area before the coming of the railways in the nineteenth century.
   c) Radio sets did not become common until the 1920s, and there was no widespread ownership of television before the 1950s.
   d) Elizabeth I and her government were worried about the possibility of invasion by Spain.
   Using these statements and any ideas which you or your teacher may have, can you work out why people were afraid of vagabonds at that time?

Different classes of pauper. (The word *pauper* means a poor person who is receiving help from his or her parish.)

Able-bodied: those who were healthy and able to work.

Sturdy beggars: those who were healthy but refused to work, preferring to wander the roads as vagabonds.

Impotent poor: those who were not able to look after themselves – the sick, the old, orphans, and children whose parents were in need of help.

The extract from the Poor Law Act shows how the government wanted the parish authorities to treat the 'sturdy beggars' – those whom they believed could work, but avoided it! The numbers of vagabonds had increased alarmingly during the sixteenth century, and the government was extremely worried by the problems which they created.

What the extract from the Poor Law does not tell you is what they had decided to do about the sick and the old – the 'impotent poor'. Elizabeth and her government were trying to create a system of poor relief which was the same all over the country. They also wanted to deal with the different types of poor in different ways. Each parish was to look after its own poor, and, to enable it to do this, a poor rate had to be collected. Men were to be appointed as 'overseers of the poor', and their job was to decide how much money was needed for poor relief. They then had to see how much each householder was able to pay and to collect the money. After that, they would meet the paupers who asked for help each week, and they would decide whether or not they needed help. The impotent poor would be given relief; the able-bodied poor who lived in the parish would be given work to do. The vagabonds would be punished severely and sent on their way. You can see some of the punishments which were thought up for wandering beggars in the pictures on the next page. It seems that a good deal of thought was put into these punishments! Would such trouble have been taken, do you think, if there had not been so many vagabonds?

Problems of poor relief

Elizabeth I did not manage to stop people from needing help from their parishes, and she did not succeed in making every area of the country treat their poor in the same way. What she did do was to create

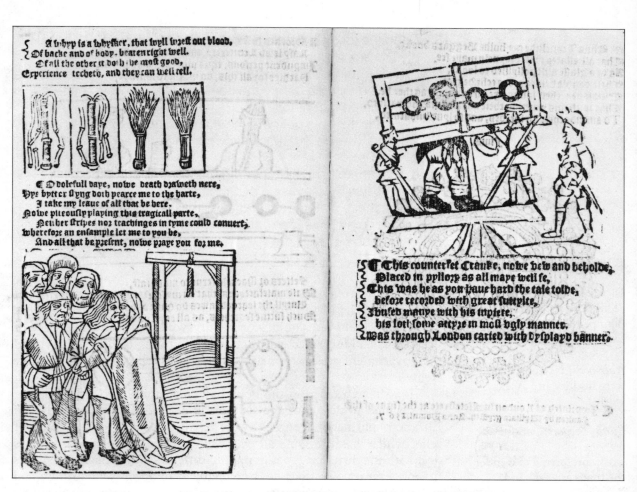

Above: *16th-century illustrations of punishments for beggars*

Right: *A persistent beggar is publicly hanged (17th-century woodcut)*

a basic system for looking after the poor, based on the parishes. Many parishes then found out how they could best look after their own poor, and between 1601 and the middle of the nineteenth century, many different solutions were tried. Some of these were laid down by Act of Parliament for all areas; others were attempts by groups of people in particular areas to meet the needs of their own parishes. Their efforts were made all the more difficult in the late eighteenth and early nineteenth centuries by a dramatic rise in the population and the enormous changes in the lives of the labouring poor brought about by the Industrial Revolution.

One of the main problems was money. In the sixteenth and seventeenth centuries, there was no such thing as income tax, which today provides some of the money used to support those who cannot support themselves. In the system of poor relief set up by Elizabeth I, the only way to get more money to support more paupers was to collect more from those in the parish who were not themselves paupers! This made those who had to pay very angry, particularly when people who did not belong to their parish claimed relief!

The Act of Settlement

Governments recognised that people did not want to support paupers from parishes other than their own. An Act of Parliament was passed in 1662, in the reign of Charles II, which allowed overseers to send away from their parish anyone who was likely to need support and who did not have 'settlement' there. A person was said to have a 'settlement' in a parish if he was born there, had moved there to take up an apprenticeship or had worked there for more than a year. A woman became 'settled' in her husband's parish. However, people could move from their parish of settlement. If a man wanted a job in another parish, he would be given a certificate which said that his own parish would have him back if ever he needed poor relief. This Settlement Law was partly intended to prevent people from moving from parish to parish in the hope of finding one which was really generous to the poor.

What often happened after this Act became law was that any strangers who arrived in the parish would be thrown out again if they looked as though they might need relief. The law was later changed so that only those who had actually begun to get relief from a parish other than their own could be removed. There was a nasty sting in the tail, though; everyone receiving relief had to wear a special badge.

Many paupers who were too old or too ill to look after themselves, or who had nowhere to live, were put into places known as almshouses or poorhouses. These are the old names; they also became known by a name which came to be only too familiar in the nineteenth and twentieth centuries – workhouses.

Were the poor always badly treated?

It would be a mistake to believe that the poor were always treated cruelly. Elizabeth I's government did try to make sure that those who really could not work were given clothes, food and somewhere to live. The ones who suffered were those who refused to work, or who pretended to be ill in order to get relief – and there were a lot of them! Those who could not find a job also suffered. The authorities of the sixteenth, seventeenth and eighteenth centuries very often believed that it was people's own fault if they could not get a job; all they had to do, they thought, was to look for one! Many better-off people believed that being poor was a sort of punishment for being sinful or lazy. These people did not approve of handing out money to the poor, especially when they had to provide the money.

Nevertheless, many parishes did try to provide as well as they could for their poor, as this section from the overseers' accounts for June and July, 1693, from Hitchin in Hertfordshire, shows.

June 26th	p[ai]d Rob[ert] Bonfield in distr[es]s		0	2	0
	p[ai]d Widd[ow] Sherman in distr[es]s		0	0	6
	p[ai]d Widd[ow] Martin for Woods Child		0	1	0
	p[ai]d Widd[ow] Willy in distr[es]s		0	2	0
	p[ai]d W[illia]m Dellow for dyetting the worke folke		0	18	0
	p[ai]d Jo[h]n Hanger w[i]th Woods Child apprentice		2	10	0
	p[ai]d W[illia]m Dellow for dyetting the worke folke for 3 dayes		0	18	0
	p[ai]d W[illia]m Hudson in distr[es]s		0	1	0
	p[ai]d Yelding of Langley in distr[es]s		0	1	6
	p[ai]d Tho[mas] Watts in distr[es]s		0	0	6
	p[ai]d Widd[ow] Oakley in distr[es]s		0	0	6
	p[ai]d Jo[h]n Iszard in distr[es]s		0	1	6
	p[ai]d Fosse for Rands Child		0	1	0
July 3rd	p[ai]d Widd[ow] Martin for Woods Child		0	1	0
	p[ai]d Rob[ert] Bonfield in distr[es]s		0	2	0
	p[ai]d Widd[ow] Sherman in distr[es]s		0	0	6
	p[ai]d Geor[ge] Warner in distr[es]s		0	2	0
	p[ai]d Widd[ow] Willy in distr[es]s		0	2	0
	p[ai]d W[illia]m Dellow for dyetting the worke folke for 3 dayes		0	18	0
	p[ai]d W[illia]m Hudson in distr[es]s		0	1	0
	p[ai]d W[illia]m Dellow for dyetting the worke folke for 3 dayes		0	5	3
	p[ai]d Mrs. Godfrey for Curing Jo[h]n Iszard		0	15	0
	p[ai]d to W[illia]m Arnolds wife in distr[es]s		0	1	0

We also have a record of the food which the inmates of the poorhouse at Hemel Hempstead, Hertfordshire, ate during a week in mid-December, 1741. Although it seems very boring and unappetising, it was not so very different from the sort of food which a working family would have eaten at that time.

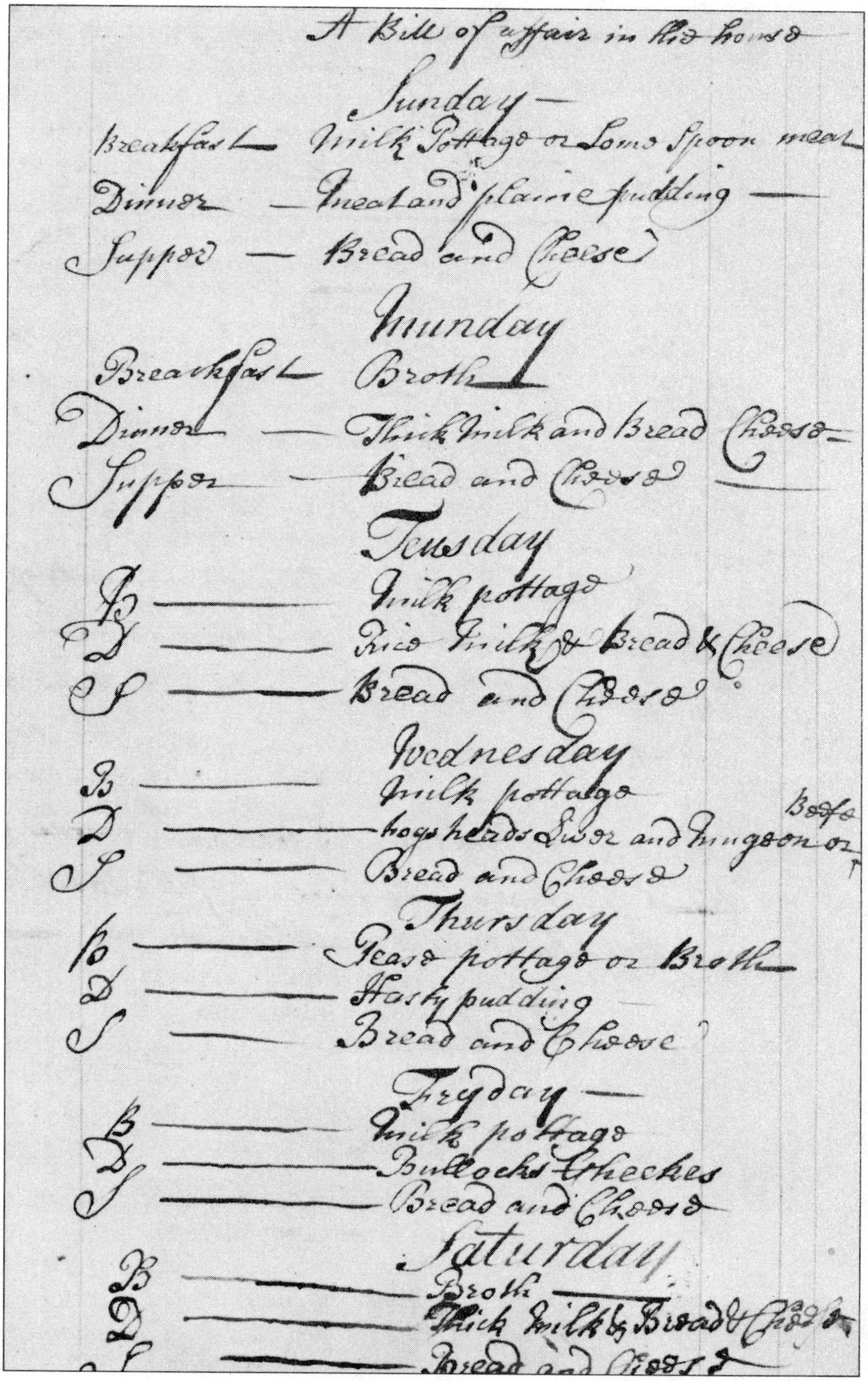

A Bill of affair in this house

Sunday —

Breakfast — Milk Pottage or some spoon meat

Dinner — meat and plaine pudding —

Supper — Bread and Cheese

Munday

Breakfast — Broth

Dinner — Thick Milk and Bread Cheese

Supper — Bread and Cheese

Teusday

B — Milk pottage

D — Rice Milk & Bread & Cheese

S — Bread and Cheese

Wednesday

B — Milk pottage

D — hogs heads Liver and lungson or Beefe

S — Bread and Cheese

Thursday

B — Peas pottage or Broth

D — Hasty pudding

S — Bread and Cheese

Fryday —

B — Milk pottage

D — Bullocks Cheeks

S — Bread and Cheese

Saturday

B — Broth

D — Thick Milk & Bread & Cheese

S — Bread and Cheese

There is no doubt that the number of people claiming relief did rise in the time between the reign of Elizabeth I and the nineteenth century. The belief that too many idle or work-shy people were getting money from the parishes led to an Act of Parliament in 1723. This set out ways in which parishes, either by themselves or in groups, could provide a workhouse where the able-bodied poor would be made to work. If the able-bodied poor refused to enter the workhouse they would '...not be entitled to ask or demand relief ... from the ... overseers of the poor in their ... parishes'. (The Workhouse Test Act, 1723.)

By 1776 there were almost 2 000 workhouses in England, each one holding between 20 and 50 inmates. The problem, still, was to differentiate between those who truly deserved and needed help, and those who (according to the authorities) were poor through their own fault.

Gilbert's Act

In 1782, the government tried to set out more clearly the different types of poor who were claiming relief, so that they could provide more suitable help for the old, the sick and the orphans in the workhouse. This Act was introduced into Parliament by Thomas Gilbert, a country gentleman and MP from Staffordshire. His main aim, however, was to enable parishes to combine into groups to build a workhouse. Before his Act was passed each group had to ask permission from Parliament if they wanted to do this. Now a poor parish could join together with a richer one to build and run a workhouse.

Gilbert's Act also made sure that, as far as possible, only the old, the sick and orphans lived in the workhouses. All the others who needed relief were given money, and they had to look after themselves. This system of 'outdoor relief' was to cost the country a good deal of money towards the end of the eighteenth century. This was especially true in the south of England, where the main occupation was farming. A rising population and changes in farming methods caused more able-bodied people to be unemployed and to seek outdoor relief. Those who did have jobs were often so badly paid that they, too, were forced to ask for help from their parishes.

William Cobbett, who travelled round southern England between 1822 and 1830, wrote about the poor farmworkers, their crumbling cottages and their despair:

> *The labourers here look as if they were half-starved.... For my own part, I really am ashamed to ride a fat horse, to have a full belly, and to have a clean shirt upon my back when I look at those wretched countrymen of mine; while I actually see them reeling with weakness; when I see their poor faces present me nothing but skin and bone....*
>
> William Cobbett: *Rural Rides*, 1831

Questions

1 What different sorts of people used to claim relief in the sixteenth, seventeenth and eighteenth centuries? (See pages 12, 14 and 16 in particular.)

2 Take each of these people in turn, and explain the sort of treatment which they would have received. In addition to the pages given in Question 1, see page 17.

3 What attitudes did better-off people have towards the different sorts of poor people?

4 The system of poor relief changed between the sixteenth century and the end of the eighteenth century. Does the fact that it changed mean that it had improved? Think about this, and try to explain your answer very carefully.

Summary of Poor Law Acts mentioned in this chapter:

1601:   Elizabeth I's last Poor Law Act.
1662:   Settlement Act.
1723:   Workhouse Test Act.
1782:   Gilbert's Act.

vestry: a committee of people in a parish, which controlled parish affairs, including the administration of poor relief

In the next chapter we shall see how the great changes of the industrial and agricultural revolutions put enormous pressure on the old ways of dealing with the poor. We shall also see how people tried to relieve these pressures until, finally, the government of the 1830s was forced to look very closely at the whole of the Old Poor Law, and to introduce new ideas in the Poor Law Amendment Act of 1834.

A   *Using the evidence: the Old Poor Law in Hertfordshire*

Poor House Cheshunt 1 Feby 1796

At a Meeting of the Committee appointed by an Order of Vestry held 14th Janry for the purpose of applying in the best manner, ~~to the Use of the Poor~~, the Rate of 6d in the Pound lately ordered to be Levied for the Use of the Labouring Poor during the present high Price of Provisions — Present

From the minutes of the Cheshunt vestry, 1 February 1796

B   The spelling in the following extract seems very odd to us, but there were not really any agreed ways of spelling most words in the eighteenth century. Even so, the clerk who wrote this seems to have been worse than most at spelling. It would help you to read the extract aloud.

Att a Vestry Hild the 23 day of Feb: 1753. It was a greed that We Hose names are under Writen Do all agree that the Churchwardens and Overseares shall In dever to inquier in to the afare of the Church Houses in order to Make a work Hous of them for the maintaince of the poor and to see that they are took care of to be In ploied and ceep in a decand maner and they are to Indever to Have in don in the best maner that they cane.
[A list of names follows; these would have been members of the vestry.]

From the minutes of the Kings Langley vestry, 23 February 1753

C   This is a letter sent by Robert Fitch to the overseers of Royston in the early nineteenth century. The year is not known, but the letter is dated 21 February.

Sir,
I have sent you my Examination in a letter. But you have sent me no word About it weather you mean to relieve me or not. But if the parrish dont believe me now I shall send my wife and five children home to the parrish for I have Enquire into the Law that you Carnt Onley take 2 of my Children into the house which is above 7 years Old for you Carnt take the Others till they are 7 years Old away from her so if you dont think proper to relive me I shall sell my things as i have told you Befor to pay my debts And i Shall Go to Sea or for a [soldier] So then you may keep them all for it seem to me that you mean to drive me to it for i Carnt meantain them with my pay. And if you will provide me a house and get me a house to live in and find me work at my trad i will com home. And then i must hav things to put into it for I ham Shore that I Sharnt have aney money to Buy any Goods whith. So i Shall Be Glad if you will send Me a Anser about it.
> *From*
> > *yours*
> > > *Robt Fitch*
> *Brasted*
> > *Kent.*

D

> **Wool Room**
>
> 1 Scale beam with planks & ropes,
> 4 lead weights, 1 sorting board & frame,
> 1 lock & key to door.
>
> **Spinning Rooms.**
>
> 1 small grate, 1 fender, 2 flat irons,
> with pads, 1 round table, 6 chairs, 2 stools,
> 1 pair of bellows, 1 broad step ladder,
> 1 smaller d.º 2 forms, 28 wheels,
> 3 reels, 3 pair of wool cards.

Part of an inventory of Royston workhouse goods, about 1800

1   The members of the vestry in Cheshunt (source **A**) are making an order about the poor rate. The minutes of the Kings Langley vestry (source **B**) give details of what the parish intended to do for their poor.

   How does source **A** help to explain any problems which men such as those in the Kings Langley vestry might have had in carrying out their intentions?

2   Read source **C**. The 'examination' to which Robert Fitch is referring is his certificate of Settlement.
   a) Can you explain why, when he is living in Kent, he is asking the overseers of a Hertfordshire parish for relief?
   b) Why does his threat that he will 'go to sea or for a soldier' amount almost to blackmail?
   c) How does Robert Fitch's letter throw light upon
      (i) the desperation of the poor?
      (ii) the resentment of the rate-payers?

3   Look at sources **B** and **D**. Source **B** describes what the parish has agreed to do for the poor. Which aspect of looking after the poor, mentioned in source **B**, is referred to in source **D**?

4   These sources do not give the impression that the poor were treated badly in Royston and Kings Langley. Why, then, do you think that so many people resented having to 'go on the parish'?

5   Do you think that these sources alone give you enough evidence to enable you to describe how the poor were treated in Hertfordshire in the eighteenth century? Explain your answer.

3

'OH PITY OUR TERRIBLE CASE'

Elizabeth I's Poor Law was made at a time when most people lived and worked in the country. It was adapted over the centuries to cope with the needs of orphans, the homeless and the unemployed and to punish those who were regarded as lazy, idle rogues. As time went on, this system was stretched more and more, until the great changes in industry and agriculture from the middle of the eighteenth century onwards stretched it almost to breaking point. It had never been intended to meet the needs of people living and working in the growing industrial towns; it was also not able to cope with the increased unemployment and poverty in the farming areas of Britain.

A growing population

Beneath all this was probably the greatest problem of all: the population was rising faster than it had ever done before. In the sixteenth century the population of England and Wales was about four million. By 1801, when the first census (official count) was taken, it had risen to nine million, and was still rising. In 1834, when the government introduced the new Poor Law system, it was fourteen million.

You can see from this graph how the population rose between 1711 and 1891:

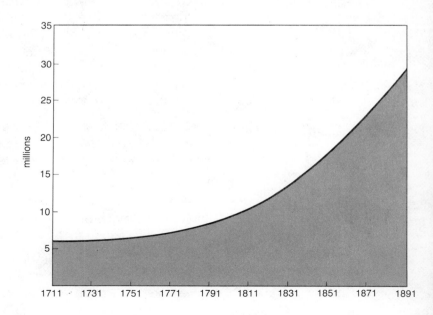

There was no central control of poor relief, and so, in the early nineteenth century, no one was able to make plans for the increased numbers of paupers and the different problems of agricultural and industrial areas.

The fast-growing, northern industrial towns did not suffer from poverty and unemployment to the same extent as the agricultural areas in the south and south-east of England. Of course, towns such as Manchester, Bradford and Sheffield had their own problems, but they could at least provide jobs in the textile mills and the ironworks, even if conditions were bad and wages low. It was the parishes in the agricultural south which had to bear the cost of increasing numbers of paupers and poverty-stricken families.

These figures (for the whole country) tell us how much money was spent on poor relief from 1776–1833:

1776	£1 520 000	1822	£5 773 000
1802	£4 078 000	1823	£5 737 000
1812	£6 676 000	1824	£5 787 000
1813	£6 295 000	1825	£5 929 000
1814	£5 419 000	1826	£6 441 000
1815	£5 725 000	1827	£6 298 000
1816	£6 911 000	1828	£6 332 000
1817	£7 871 000	1829	£6 829 000
1818	£7 517 000	1830	£6 799 000
1819	£7 330 000	1831	£7 037 000
1820	£6 959 000	1832	£6 791 000
1821	£6 359 000	1833	£6 317 000

Questions

1 Look again at the graph. Which of these sentences do you think best describes what it is telling us?
 a) The population grew rapidly in the first half of the eighteenth century and slowed down afterwards.
 b) The population grew hardly at all in the first half of the eighteenth century, grew rapidly in the second half of the eighteenth century and slowed down after that.
 c) The population grew hardly at all in the first half of the eighteenth century, grew slowly during the second half of the eighteenth century and grew rapidly during the nineteenth century.

2 a) Look again at the poor relief figures. Taking into account the fact that Britain was at war with France between 1793 and 1815, and that there were bad harvests on and off throughout the period (particularly between 1815–20), which of the following sentences best describes what was happening to the amount spent on poor relief:
  (i) The amount rose steadily from 1776 onwards.

(ii) The amount rose sharply during the war and reached a peak just before the Poor Law Amendment Act was passed in 1834.

(iii) The amount rose steadily until it reached its peak just after the war. It went down after that, but still stayed higher than it was before the war.

Find out whether your answer was right or not. Then try to explain the correct answer, using the figures and any other information which you have.

b) Which of the following conclusions could you draw from the graph and the poor relief figures? Explain your choice.

  (i) It was the war which caused poor relief to rise in cost.

  (ii) The rising population meant that there were more paupers as time went on.

  (iii) Both of these may have contributed to the problem, but I need more information before I can really say.

If you gave (iii) as your answer, what other information do you think that you need to be able to explain why the cost of poor relief rose?

Why were the farmworkers so poor?

Britain was at war with France between 1793 and 1815. In 1806, Napoleon Bonaparte, Emperor of France, put a blockade on trade with Britain, to prevent food and other goods from reaching her shores. With no competition from abroad, British farmers could raise their prices. Napoleon had intended the blockade to be a disaster for Britain, but what really happened was that many farmers made huge profits, extended their farms and prospered as never before.

The blockade did not last long, but the war disrupted trade and it was difficult to import goods, including grain. British farmers had no need to lower their prices as long as there was no foreign competition, and bad harvests from time to time ensured that prices remained high during the war. The farmers were doing well, but those who had to buy bread on which to live found it difficult to support themselves and their families because wages remained low.

High food prices obviously affected all workers, in town and country, but the farmworkers' poverty was made worse by the widespread enclosure of common and waste land in the villages of the Midlands, the south and the south-east. Enclosure did, as a matter of fact, produce more jobs, as labourers were needed on the newly enclosed farms for jobs such as hedging and ditching. The real problem was that the fast-growing population meant that even so there were not enough jobs for everyone. Poverty was made worse because enclosure led to the loss of villagers' rights to graze a cow or to collect wood on the old common land.

In addition to this, the old system of cottage industries, where families used to spin and weave wool into cloth to increase their incomes, could no longer compete with the new factories. In the north, unemployed farmworkers could at least seek, and often find, work in the factories and mills in nearby towns. In the south they had no such alternative; their only hope was to apply to the parish for poor relief.

The hand-workers

Even where industry was growing, however, poverty threatened those who, before the coming of the powered machines, had been proud and prosperous hand-weavers in the cotton textile towns of south Lancashire.

jubilee: time for celebration
lawn: fine cotton cloth

> *Four days did the weaver work, for then four days was a week, and such a week to a skilled workman brought forty shillings. Sunday, Monday and Tuesday were of course jubilee. Lawn frills gorged freely from under the wrists of his fine blue, gilt-buttoned coat. He dusted his head with white flour on Sunday, smirked, and wore a cane. Walked in clean slippers on Monday, Tuesday heard him talk war bravado . . . and get drunk. Weaving commenced gradually on Wednesday.*
>
> William Thom: *Rhymes and Recollections of a Handloom Weaver,*
> 1845

Powered machinery changed the lives of the hand-loom weavers. They could not keep up with the output of the power looms, so they too joined the ranks of the poorly paid or the unemployed, if they refused to work in a mill, as many did at first. The stocking knitters of Nottingham suffered too, when the new machinery took over from their foot-operated stocking frames. Perhaps the figures below and the ballad will help to make the misery of the hand-workers clearer.

A Wages of a hand-loom weaver in Bolton, a cotton textile town in Lancashire:

1797	1800	1805	1810	1816	1820	1824	1830
30s.	25s.	25s.	19s.	12s.	9s.	8s. 6d.	5s. 6d.

framework knitter: person who worked a foot-driven stocking frame
Sutton: in Nottinghamshire
bag-masters: middlemen who supplied materials to the knitters and collected the finished work

B *The Miseries of the Framework Knitters*

Ye kind-hearted souls, pray attend to our song,
And hear this true story which shall not be long;
Framework knitters of Sutton, how ill they are used,
And by the bag-masters how sorely abused.

Chorus
Derry down, down, down derry down.

bated: reduced

They've bated the wages so low for our work
That to gain half maintainence we slave like a Turk;
When we ask for our money comes paper and string,
Dear beef and bad mutton or some suchlike thing.

Bad weights and bad measures are frequently used –
Oppressive extortion – thus sorely abused;
Insulted and robbed, too – we mention no names –
But pluck up our spirits and bowl in their frames.

Good people, oh pity our terrible case,
Pray take no offence though we visit this place;
We crave your assistance and pray for our foes,
Oh may they find mercy when this life we lose.

This ballad first appeared in the early nineteenth century

C

Above: *A hand-weaver at work*

Right: *Power-loom weavers*

D

Questions

1 Which aspects of their old lives do you think the hand-weavers would have missed most when they fell on hard times? Use the extract from William Thom's book to help you to answer this.

2 Can you think of any reasons why the hand-weavers might not have wanted to accept work as power-loom weavers in a mill? You will find that sources **B**, **C** and **D** will help you.

3 List the complaints which the frame-knitters were making in their ballad (source **B**). Which of these complaints do you think was the most serious? Give reasons for your answer.

4 Why might people who had been hand-weavers or frame-knitters *especially* resent 'going on the parish' and seeking relief?

5 William Thom's book is about a hand-weaver's memories. The ballad – a popular 'protest' song – was probably used as a fund raiser for workers whose pay dropped or who lost their jobs. Does this mean that the ballad is likely to be less reliable than the book as evidence of the poverty of the time?

Poverty in the northern industrial towns

There were hundreds of mills in the woollen textile towns of the West Riding of Yorkshire and the cotton textile towns of south Lancashire. Although the mills provided jobs for those who lived in and around these areas, people often had to live and work in intolerable conditions. The picture of Bradford below gives an idea of the crowded and smoky surroundings in which factory workers had to live. The pictures of Birmingham on the next page also show you what an industrial town was like. Remember too what you read in chapter 1 about the dreadful poverty of people in nineteenth century towns.

A view of Bradford from the south east, 1841

Sketches of Birmingham slums from The Illustrated London News, *mid-19th century*

The textile workers of the north also suffered from periods of unemployment when there was a slump in trade, or business was slack. They would then have to ask for relief from their parish overseers. At any time, too, a family could be hit by sickness or death, and have no means of making up for lost wages except by 'going on the parish'. Old age often brought poverty, even after a lifetime of working, for there were no pensions, and the children could not always afford to look after their parents. All of this caused more people to ask for relief, in the north as well as in the south.

Questions

William Cobbett (see chapter 2, page 18) was an outspoken critic of the dreadful conditions in which people had to live and work in town and country. He wrote this in a journal which he edited:

. . . before this system, which has corrupted everything, was known in this country, there were none of these places called Manufactories. To speak of these places with any degree of patience is impossible. It is to be a despicable hypocrite, to

*pretend to believe that the slaves in the West Indies are not
better off than the slaves in these manufactories.*

*Some of these lords of the loom have in their employ
thousands of miserable creatures. In the cotton-spinning
work, these creatures are kept, fourteen hours in each day,
locked up, summer and winter, in a heat of from Eighty to
Eightyfour degrees. The rules which they are subjected to are
such as no negroes were ever subjected to.*

William Cobbett: the *Political Register*, 20 November 1824

Cobbett mentions here the slaves in the West Indies. There was
obviously a comparison to be made between the slaves on the
sugar plantations of the West Indies and the workers in the
factories and mills in the industrial towns of Britain. The cartoon
on the next page, which makes that comparison, was published in
a magazine in Britain in 1832.

1 What name do we use today for Cobbett's 'Manufactories'?

2 Would you say that Cobbett was praising or criticising the
factory system? Which parts of the extract would you use to
show this?

Reform Bill 1832: gave the vote to middle-class people but not to working-class people

Magna Carta 1215: charter signed by King John, which promised certain rights, mainly to the nobility

3 Look carefully at the cartoon. The slaves in the West Indies were owned by their masters, and had no rights as human beings. Some of them may have had kind masters, and lived in good conditions. What different points of view is the cartoon trying to put over?

4 For what purpose do you think the cartoon was drawn?

5 With which point(s) of view in the cartoon would William Cobbett have agreed?

6 Who do *you* think was better off – the British factory worker or the West Indian slave? Think about your answer very carefully before writing it down. You could also use the pictures on pages 27, 28 and 29 to help you with this.

4 PROBLEMS AND PROTEST

Although many people found jobs in the factories and on the newly enclosed farms, there was still, as we have seen, a great deal of unemployment and poverty. The 1790s were a time of bad harvests and high bread prices. You saw in chapter 2 how the cost of poor relief went up between 1776 and 1802. This worried the rate-payers and the parish authorities who had to cope with the problem. It also worried the government. To have discontented working people, large numbers of unemployed and angry rate-payers could mean trouble.

The allowance system

The Elizabethan Poor Law had made the parish responsible for looking after the poor. Individual parishes tried to cope with the problem of poverty in their own way at the end of the eighteenth century. A parish in Cambridgeshire tried out a system to help low-paid workers as early as 1785, even before the French war had begun. We know most, however, about a system which was begun in the village of Speenhamland in Berkshire in 1795. We know about this partly because many parishes in the south of England copied this scheme, and partly because it was described in a very early book on the state of the poor in England, by Sir Frederick Eden. This book has provided a lot of information for people who want to study poverty.

The idea behind the Speenhamland system was that a person's wages would be made up to the amount which the magistrates thought was sufficient, based on the price of a gallon loaf. If the person asking for help was a married man, the amount given was also based on the size of his family. The parish would make up the difference between the wages and the amount which the magistrates thought a person needed. Nothing was said about what their actual wages should be.

This extract from Sir Frederick Eden's book, *The State of the Poor* (1797), explains how the Speenhamland system worked:

Income should be	For a Man	For a Single Woman	For a Man and Wife	With 1 Child	With 2 Children
When the gallon loaf is 1s 0d	3s 0d	2s 0d	4s 6d	6s 0d	7s 6d
When the gallon loaf is 1s 1d	3s 3d	2s 1d	4s 10d	6s 5d	8s 0d
When the gallon loaf is 1s 2d	3s 6d	2s 2d	5s 2d	6s 10d	8s 6d
When the gallon loaf is 1s 3d	3s 9d	2s 3d	5s 6d	7s 3d	9s 0d
When the gallon loaf is 1s 4d	4s 0d	2s 4d	5s 10d	7s 8d	9s 6d
When the gallon loaf is 1s 5d	4s 0d	2s 5d	5s 11d	7s 10d	9s 9d
When the gallon loaf is 1s 6d	4s 3d	2s 6d	6s 3d	8s 3d	10s 3d
When the gallon loaf is 1s 7d	4s 3d	2s 7d	6s 4d	8s 5d	10s 6d
When the gallon loaf is 1s 8d	4s 6d	2s 8d	6s 8d	8s 10d	11s 0d
When the gallon loaf is 1s 9d	4s 6d	2s 9d	6s 9d	9s 0d	11s 3d
When the gallon loaf is 1s 10d	4s 9d	2s 10d	7s 1d	9s 5d	11s 9d

Loaf weighing 8 lb 11 oz

What effect might this system have had on
a)   employers and wages?
b)   those who had to claim relief from the parish in this way?

Schemes like this one from Berkshire were much needed during the war against France between 1793 and 1815. At this time, as we have seen in chapter 3, the price of corn (and therefore of bread) rose. Many parishes in the south of England adopted the Speenhamland scheme, or one like it, although it did not spread to the north, where the problems of poverty in industrial towns were quite different.

The Corn Law

The ending of the war did not bring improvements for the unemployed and the poorly paid. There was a slump in industry and agriculture; bad weather caused more bad harvests; returning soldiers and sailors added to the numbers of the unemployed. Wages remained low and the government, under the Prime Minister, Lord Liverpool, made matters worse for the poor by stopping foreign corn from coming in to Britain unless the cost of wheat grown at home was at the famine-level price. This meant that, unless British corn cost 80 shillings (£4) per quarter or more, no foreign corn was to be allowed in, and farmers would not be forced to lower their prices in order to sell. This might seem ridiculous, to appear to raise prices so that bread was dear and people could not afford to buy it, and this was just how poor people saw it. The government, however, had to listen to the MPs, all of whom were landowners who were afraid that their profits, so great during the war, would drop once foreign corn could come into Britain again. What actually happened was not as bad as the people had feared. If you look at the chart below, you can see that the price of wheat went up and down in the years after 1815. Prices were never as high again as they had been during the war years, though they were higher, on average, than they had been before the war.

quarter: 560lb (25kg) or a quarter of a ton

Annual average wheat prices in England and Wales, 1771–1850

Period	Average for period	Highest price	Lowest price
1771–5	51.5s	54/3	48/7
1776–80	40.2	46/11	34/8
1781–5	48.6	54/3	43/1
1786–90	47.2	54/9	40/0
1791–5	53.6	75/2	43/0
1796–1800	73.7	113/10	51/10

Period	Average for period	Highest price	Lowest price
1801–1805	80.0	119/6	62/3
1806–10	88.0	106/5	75/4
1811–15	97.2	126/6	65/7
1816–20	80.8	96/11	67/10
1821–5	57.3	68/6	44/7
1826–30	61.6	66/3	58/6
1831–5	52.6	66/4	39/4
1836–40	61.2	70/8	48/6
1841–5	54.8	64/4	50/1
1846–50	51.9	69/9	40/3

What working people resented about this Corn Law was that Parliament was supporting the landowners and the farmers, while the labouring classes, whatever the price of bread, had no help to relieve their low wages and appalling conditions at home and at work. Those whose wages were so low that they could not support themselves, and those who were unemployed had, in their own eyes, the worst deal of all. Not only did they share the poor living conditions of the working labourers, they also had the shame of 'going on the parish' if they were to live at all. Anger and frustration turned to violence in many places, and there were riots and protests against the Corn Laws.

Bread riots in London, 1815. These people were protesting against the Corn Laws

The Roundsman System, and the labour rate

Other schemes to reduce the amount of money spent on poor relief were tried out. One of these was called the Roundsman System. There were several different Roundsman Systems which various parishes developed, but the basic idea was that unemployed labourers would go round the parish looking for work. A man would receive perhaps 6d. (about $2\frac{1}{2}$ pence) per day from his employer; the parish would add a small amount – perhaps 4d. (about $1\frac{1}{2}$ pence) per day.

Some parishes set up a system known as the labour rate. Rate-payers paid a separate rate in addition to the ordinary poor rate; employers could choose either to pay their share of this rate or to use it to pay labourers at the going rate for labour in the parish.

All that these schemes really did was to complicate the Poor Law system. Some help was, of course, given to the poor, but although parish after parish might try out different methods of coping with poverty and the rising cost of poor relief, what they could not do was reduce the number of paupers and low-paid labourers. Some people criticised the idea of giving financial help to the poor. An Anglican clergyman, Thomas Malthus, claimed that the system of poor relief in England encouraged people to marry early and to have large families since it was those with several children who received the most money. Others were worried about the effects of poverty upon the morals of the paupers; they feared that they would no longer want to work, and would cease to respect their betters.

The 'Swing' riots

Many people's worst fears were realised in 1830 when, in many parts of the country, but mainly in the southern counties, agricultural labourers erupted into violence and hay-rick burning. They had been driven to the limits of their endurance by low wages, poor conditions and the belief that the new machinery, such as the threshing machines, were putting them out of work. They could not show their feelings by voting in local or parliamentary elections, as the labouring classes had not yet been given the right to vote. Their only outlet was violence, if no one would speak for them.

These 'Swing' riots (named after the man whom they claimed to be their leader) probably hastened the setting up of a Royal Commission to investigate how the Poor Law worked. It was the report of this Commission, published in February 1834, which led to the Poor Law Amendment Act of April 1834.

Questions

1   The man shown in source **A** is one of the rick-burners who took part in the 'Swing' riots. Is the cartoonist sympathising with the man or not? Give reasons for your answer.

A *A cartoon from* Punch

B *A poster advertising a reward in Essex, 1830*

2 How does source **B** help us to understand why the 'Swing' riots made better-off people even more determined to contribute less to the poor rate?

Using the evidence

1 Look back at the list of figures on page 23 and the chart of wheat prices on pages 32–3. Which of the following conclusions fit in with the information given in these sources?
   a) Wheat prices were highest when the most money was spent on poor relief.
   b) Wheat prices were highest in the last years of the war, when money spent on poor relief was still rising.
   c) Wheat prices were continuing to rise throughout the period, as was the amount spent on poor relief.

   Now look back to Question **2b** on page 24. Does the information on the price of wheat give any further help in explaining the rising cost of poor relief in the early nineteenth century?

THE LIFE OF A LABOURER

CONTENT HAVING FOOD & RAIMENT

BEGGARD BY MISGOVERNMENT AND
RECEIVING ALMS OF THE PARISH

IN IGNORANCE TRIES TO
RIGHT HIMSELF AND GETS

PUNISHMENT IN ENGLAND FOR
A BLOODLESS RIOT.

These drawings date from the worst years of rioting by agricultural labourers. They show an imaginary labourer, but they do tell a story and give some idea of how people felt about the problem of poverty at that time.

a) Try to explain this story from the point of view of (i) the farm labourer, and (ii) the authorities who condemned him to death.

b) Do you think that the artist was on the labourer's side or not? Explain your answer.

c) Why do you think men were hanged for smashing machinery?

3 In 1831, the amount of poor relief paid out per head of the population was:
2s. $11\frac{1}{2}$d. in Bradford,
5s. $7\frac{1}{2}$d. in the whole of the West Riding of Yorkshire,
4s. $4\frac{3}{4}$d. in Lancashire,
16s. 6d. in Wiltshire,
18s. $3\frac{1}{4}$d. in Suffolk.
Use the information and evidence given in this chapter to explain these figures.

5

THE NEW POOR LAW

In the years after 1601, when Elizabeth I's government had put together all the laws for looking after the poor into one great Act, the methods of looking after the poor came to differ from place to place. The number of paupers grew, especially during the late eighteenth and early nineteenth centuries, and ways had to be found of giving relief to those who needed it. The trouble was that all this cost a good deal of money which had to be raised from the rate-payers of each parish. The rate-payers disliked having to pay out so much money, and their attitude towards the poor hardened. Many believed that there were far too many able-bodied paupers who were receiving money from their parishes when they could – and should – have been working. The 'Swing' riots of 1830 and 1831 increased feelings of hostility towards the poor. The only answer, it seemed, was to change the system, and to find a way of looking after those who really needed help without over-burdening the rate-payers.

The Royal Commission, 1832–34

In February, 1832, the government set up a commission to find out how the present Poor Law system was working, and to make suggestions as to how it could be changed and improved. There were eight commissioners, including Charles Blomfield, Bishop of London, who was the chairman, and the economist Nassau Senior. There were 26 assistant commissioners, of which the most energetic and hard-working was Edwin Chadwick, a journalist who was to become the most famous figure in the history of the workhouse. Within a year, Chadwick was made a commissioner, and it was he and Nassau Senior who were responsible for writing the 300-page *Report of the Royal Commission*.

The commissioners prepared this report from a mass of information collected by the assistant commissioners on visits to some 3000 parishes. However, they had already made up their minds about what the report should say, so they hoped to read that it was outdoor relief which was the cause of idleness amongst the poor. They also hoped to find that the parish poorhouses were inefficient because each parish, big or small, ran its own establishment.

The assistant commissioners discovered all sorts of workhouses and all sorts of conditions. They had many criticisms to make of the way in which the larger, more comfortable workhouses encouraged the able-bodied to be idle. Sir Francis Head, reporting from Kent, wrote about a workhouse in which he found 'a room full of sturdy labourers in hobnailed boots and smock-frocks, sitting round a stove with their

Above: The workhouse at Eversholt, Bedfordshire, in the early 19th century. This was one of the old-style workhouses, but it looks as if it was kept in good repair. Notice the stocks outside: as well as being looked after, paupers were sometimes punished

Right: The parish workhouse of St James's, London, at the beginning of the 19th century. The commissioners said that it was too luxurious and encouraged idleness

faces scorched and half-roasted'. As he passed 'they never rose from their seats, and had generally an over-fed, a mutinous and an insubordinate appearance'.

The report was published in February 1834. The main criticism of the old system was that there were too many able-bodied people – paupers and low-paid labourers – claiming relief. In the words of the report: 'The great source of abuse is outdoor relief afforded to the able-bodied.'

The commissioners proposed that there should be a single system of poor relief throughout the country, but even more important was this proposal:

> ... except as to medical attendance ... all relief whatever to able-bodied persons or to their families, otherwise than in well-regulated workhouses ... shall be declared unlawful, and shall cease....

If this suggestion was carried out, it would mean that there would be no more outdoor relief for the able-bodied. Instead, there would be a system of 'indoor' relief, based on workhouses. The only sort of outdoor relief which would be given to them would be medical attention.

The Commission recommended that all the parishes in the country should be grouped together into 'unions', on the lines of the existing combinations of parishes set up under Gilbert's Act (see page 18). This would enable rich parishes to help poorer ones, and would ensure that there was a big enough workhouse to cope with the paupers in each union. It was important that it should be run properly, so the commissioners proposed that there should be a central Poor Law Commission to control the system and to enforce the regulations. Each union would have a Board of Guardians of the Poor, to be elected by the rate-payers.

The important point about these workhouses was that they had to be able to support those who genuinely could not look after themselves, such as the sick and the old, but they also had to be so unattractive that the able-bodied poor would have to be totally destitute and desperate before they would want to enter them. The report put it in this way:

eligible: desirable

> The first and most essential of all conditions ... is that his [the able-bodied pauper's] situation on the whole shall not be made really or apparently so eligible as the situation of the independent labourer of the lowest class.

We shall see later what was done to make the workhouses so unattractive that paupers would enter them only as a last resort. We must now see how far the recommendations of the commissioners were carried out in the Poor Law Amendment Act, which became law in August 1834.

Sir Edwin Chadwick, who was said to be 'quarrelsome, self-important, disloyal when convinced he was right, unshakable to the point of obstinacy....' Can this portrait help us to understand the sort of man he was?

The Poor Law Amendment Act

The Poor Law Amendment Act did not set down a detailed system of poor relief. What it did was to explain the principle of indoor relief in a workhouse, and to set out a way of enforcing this. There was to be a Central Poor Law Commission, which would see to the organisation of relief throughout the country. This commission was to consist of three commissioners who would introduce and supervise the new system.

The chairman of the commission was Thomas Frankland Lewis, a former Tory MP. The other two commissioners were John Shaw Lefevre, a barrister, and George Nicholls, who had been an overseer of the poor in Southwell, Nottinghamshire. Nicholls had set up a workhouse which had been run on lines similar to those laid down in the Act, and so he was to play a major part in the setting up of the new system. The Secretary to the Commissioners was Edwin Chadwick, whose view of the New Poor Law was that it was like 'a cold bath – unpleasant in contemplation but invigorating in its effects'.

Edwin Chadwick's influence over the setting up of the new Poor Law system was enormous. He had a passion for order and efficiency, and the way in which the unions and the workhouses were to be run reflected his approach to his work.

Under the new system parishes were to be grouped into unions. Each union was to have an elected Board of Guardians, who had to organise or build a workhouse, and see to its administration. All paupers who could not support themselves, and who did not qualify for outdoor relief, would go into the workhouse. There would be separate wards in each workhouse for the different classes of pauper. These had been set out by the commissioners in their report as:

1 The aged and really impotent.
2 The children.
3 The able-bodied females.
4 The able-bodied males.

The 1834 report had stated that each 'class' would be better off in a separate workhouse; the Act said that there should be one workhouse for all. The Act did not forbid outdoor relief, as the report had recommended, but it did say this:

> *... it shall be lawful for the Commissioners, by such rules, orders or regulations as they may think fit, to declare to what extent and for what period the relief to be given to able-bodied persons and their families in any particular parish or union may be administered out of the workhouse ... by payments in money or with food or clothing....*

It was left to the commissioners to decide how to reduce or abolish outdoor relief. It was abolished, union by union, when they thought the time was right. It was, however, hoped that by making outdoor relief more difficult to get, and by ensuring that the workhouses did not offer the poor desirable and attractive accommodation, people would be forced to look for employment and to support themselves as far as possible. It was this principle of 'less eligibility' which made the workhouse into a sort of 'test', for only those who were really without any means of support would want to enter it.

The commissioners, based at Somerset House in London, issued rules for the carrying out of the new Poor Law, and saw to the organisation of the unions and the handing over of the administration of the poor to the local Boards of Guardians. They had expected opposition to the grouping into unions from the parishes, so the Act had allowed the rates for poor relief to continue to be collected by each parish. What they had probably not expected was the extent of the opposition to the new law, which came mainly (but not solely) from the northern industrial towns.

Using the evidence

The main proposals of the Royal Commission were:

1   That each class of pauper should be treated in the same way all over the country.

2   That there should be no outdoor relief for the able-bodied and their families.

3   That each union of parishes should have a workhouse for the able-bodied poor who claimed relief. These should be set to work under the strictest discipline, in order to test that they really did not have any other means of support.

4   That when the able-bodied pauper was in the workhouse, his standard of living there should be worse than that of the lowest class of labourer who supported himself.

5   That the old people who were also sick and the children should be looked after in separate institutions, and not in the workhouse with the able-bodied paupers.

Now look at the picture of St James's workhouse on page 39, and the extracts from the Poor Law Report on page 40.

1   a) Which of these sources help to explain why the commissioners decided on point 4 in the list above?

    b) Find the parts of the written sources which contain any of the proposals in the list above. Write out the extract from the source and the proposal which it contains side by side in a table.

2   Look again at the extract from the Poor Law Amendment Act on page 41. In what ways does this extract differ from the recommendations in the commissioners' report (see page 40)?

6

THE NEW STARVATION LAW?

There were, as we have seen, a number of important ideas which lay behind the Poor Law Amendment Act. Two of these were particularly important. These were, firstly, that there should be a national system of poor relief, so that the different types of pauper would be treated in a similar way everywhere; and secondly, that the workhouses, which were to be the main source of relief for the destitute poor, were to be unpleasant enough to stop the idle, able-bodied poor from applying to enter. Both these ideas proved difficult to carry out. Different conditions of employment had led to different parishes developing their own systems of poor relief in the old days. In much the same way, not every union of parishes could follow the rules laid down by the Poor Law Commission after 1834. The other problem was that the harsh rules which the Poor Law Commission laid down for the workhouses made life miserable for those who, through force of circumstances, had to live there. The workhouse became known as the 'Bastille', after the prison in Paris where French kings used to keep their prisoners before the French Revolution in 1789.

Rules for the workhouse

It was some time before the commissioners were able to form the whole of England and Wales into unions. They sent assistant commissioners into each county to carry this out. The south of England was the first to be organised into unions of parishes. It was here that the poor rate had been very high. The commissioners' report had made it clear that they thought this was because so many able-bodied paupers were claiming outdoor relief.

The Boards of Guardians were directed to stop the payment of outdoor relief to the able-bodied poor, to set up workhouses and to see to all aspects of poor relief. The commissioners issued very strict rules for the workhouses. Families were to be split up, which was perhaps the worst aspect of living there. The classification of paupers was even more strict than the report had recommended (see page 41).

Class 1. *Men infirm through age or any other cause.*
Class 2. *Able-bodied men, and youths above the age of 15 years.*
Class 3. *Boys above the age of 7 years, and under that of 15.*
Class 4. *Women infirm through age or any other cause.*
Class 5. *Able-bodied women, and girls above the age of 15 years.*
Class 6. *Girls above the age of 7 years, and under that of 15.*
Class 7. *Children under 7 years of age.*

From rules drawn up by the commissioners in their
First Annual Report, 1835

A women's ward in a union workhouse in about 1843. The ward looks clean but bare and comfortless. Notice that one woman has two children with her. Perhaps this was when parents were allowed to see their children for a short time (see page 45)

Every aspect of a pauper's life in the workhouse was to be organised. Meals, bed-times, work (with no pay), education for the children and general behaviour were all regulated in great detail by the commissioners. Here are some extracts from the Rules of Conduct, laid down in the years immediately after 1834:

As soon as a pauper is admitted, he shall be placed in some room for the reception of paupers, to be termed 'the receiving ward', and shall there remain until examined by the medical officer for the workhouse. Before being removed from the receiving ward, the pauper shall be thoroughly cleansed, and shall be clothed in workhouse dress, and the clothes which he wore at the time of his admission shall be purified, and deposited in a place for that purpose, with the pauper's name affixed. Such clothes shall be restored to the pauper when he leaves the workhouse.

To each class shall be assigned that ward or separate building and yard which may be best fitted for the reception of such a class, and each class of pauper shall remain therein, without communication with those of any other class.

Provided: that if for any special reason it shall at any time appear to the Board of Guardians to be desirable to depart from the regulations in respect of any married couple, being paupers of the first and fourth classes, the Guardians shall be at liberty to resolve that such a couple shall have a sleeping apartment separate from those of other paupers.

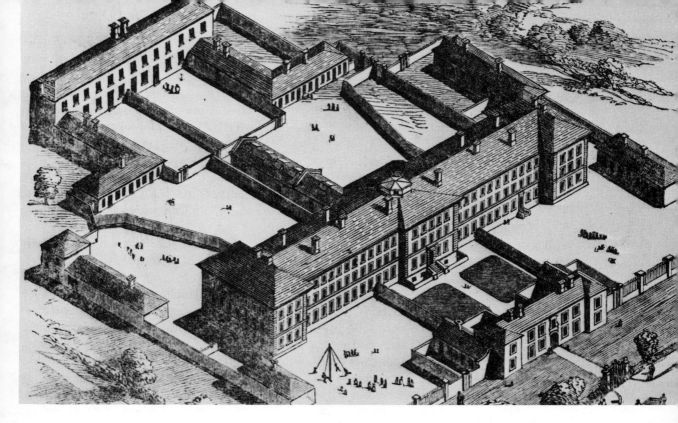

Fulham and Hammersmith workhouse in London (1849) shows the sort of building which the commissioners hoped would be built in most unions. It has accommodation for the various classes of pauper in different wards. Walls divided each class very firmly from the other classes. The children's swing was, perhaps, not typical of most workhouses!

The master of the workhouse (subject to any regulations to be made by the Board of Guardians and approved by the Poor Law Commissioners) shall allow the father or mother of any child in the same workhouse to have an interview with such child at some one time in each day.

And the Board of Guardians shall make arrangements for permitting the members of the same family who may be in different workhouses to have occasional interviews with each other, at such times and in such manner as may best suit the discipline of the several workhouses.

All the paupers in the workhouse, except the sick and insane, and the paupers of the first, fourth and seventh classes, shall rise, be set to work, leave off work, and go to bed at the times mentioned in the Form marked A.

FORM (A)

	Time of Rising	Interval for Breakfast	Time for Work	Interval for Dinner	Time for Work	Interval for Supper	Time for going to Bed
From 25th March to 29th September	¼ before 6	From ½ past 6 to 7	From 7 to 12	From 12 to 1	From 1 to 6	From 6 to 7	8 o'clock
From 29th September to 25th March	¼ before 7	From ½ past 7 to 8	From 8 to 12	From 12 to 1	From 1 to 6	From 6 to 7	8 o'clock

From rules drawn up by the commissioners in their Annual Reports between 1835 and 1841

An illustration by George Cruickshank for Oliver Twist. *The book was first published in 1838*

The commissioners were not trying to be deliberately cruel. For example, they said quite clearly in their rules that no young boy should be beaten by anyone but the schoolmaster or the master of the workhouse; that no young girl should ever be beaten; that no child under 12 should be punished by being kept alone overnight, or in a dark room. Most workhouses provided a better standard of living than a labourer would have in his own cottage, and the food was better, despite what Charles Dickens tells us in *Oliver Twist*!

Much of the food which the paupers ate was cheap carbohydrate such as potato, bread or suet pudding, but they would have meat three or four times a week, and cheese for breakfast or supper which provided protein. You can see from the dietary for able-bodied paupers at Stafford workhouse that amounts of food were quite large. Imagine eating 14 ounces of suet pudding!

There must have been workhouses in which the master did not keep to the dietary, and gave paupers far less food of very poor quality. There were certainly rumours and reports of starved paupers, as in the famous case at the Andover workhouse, reported in 1846. Apparently the paupers were so hungry that they gnawed the bones which they were breaking as part of their work. It seems, however, that the Andover union was particularly harsh towards even the impotent poor. When an old and almost blind man of 70 asked for relief, he was

DIETARY for able-bodied Men and Women.

		BREAKFAST		DINNER				SUPPER			OLD PEOPLE of 60 Years of Age and upwards, may be allowed 1oz. of Tea, 7oz. of Sugar, and 5oz. of Butter per Week, in lieu of Gruel for Breakfast, if deemed expedient to make this change.
		Bread	Gruel	Cooked Meat with Vegetables.*	Lobscouse	Soup with Vegetables.*	Suet Pudding.	Bread	Cheese	Broth Thick'ned	
		oz.	Pints.	oz.	Pints.	Pints.	oz.	oz.	oz.	Pints.	
Sunday	Men	7	1½	6	—	—	—	5	—	1½	
	Women	6	1½	5	—	—	—	4	—	1½	
Monday	Men	7	1½	—	—	1½	—	6	2	—	CHILDREN under Nine Years of Age to be allowed Bread and Milk for their Breakfast and Supper, or Gruel when Milk cannot be obtained, also such proportions of the Dinner Diet as may be requisite for their respective ages.
	Women	6	1½	—	—	1½	—	5	2	—	
Tuesday	Men	7	1½	—	—	—	14	6	2	—	
	Women	6	1½	—	—	—	12	5	2	—	
Wednesday	Men	7	1½	6	—	—	—	5	—	1½	
	Women	6	1½	5	—	—	—	4	—	1½	
Thursday	Men	7	1½	—	—	1½ (Pea Soup)	—	6	2	—	CHILDREN above Nine Years of Age to be allowed the same quantities as Women.
	Women	6	1½	—	—	1½	—	5	2	—	
Friday	Men	7	1½	—	2	—	—	6	2	—	SICK to be Dieted as directed by the Medical Officer.
	Women	6	1½	—	2	—	—	5	2	—	
Saturday	Men	7	1½	—	—	—	14	6	2	—	
	Women	6	1½	—	—	—	12	5	2	—	

"SOUP" made in the proportion of One Pound of Beef or Mutton to One Gallon of Water, with Vegetables.

"PEAS SOUP" made in the proportion of One Pound of Beef or Mutton and One Pint of Peas to One Gallon of Water.

*The VEGETABLES are EXTRA, and not included in the above specified.

told to do some work before he would be given any money. The Chairman of the Guardians also tended to put anyone who asked for relief in the workhouse, whatever their situation.

The work provided for the able-bodied in the workhouse was often monotonous and useless, such as breaking stones or bones, or oakum picking (unravelling and removing the tar from rope). Paupers who refused to work were punished, as you can see in the document below.

From the records of Stafford union workhouse

COUNTY OF Stafford,} **Be it Remembered,** That on the *twenty second* day of *November* — in the *seventh* — year of our Sovereign Lady Queen Victoria, and in the year of our Lord one thousand eight hundred and *forty three* — at *Forebridge* — in the County of Stafford, *John Brown of Stafford in the County of Stafford Labourer* — convicted before *me, one* of Her Majesty's Justices of the Peace for the said County, upon ~~the oath of~~ *his own confession* — for that *he* the said *John Brown being a person* ~~on the~~ *maintained in the* ~~legal~~ *Workhouse of* ~~at~~ the *Stafford* ~~of~~ *Union such* — ~~in the said County~~ *Workhouse being a Public Workhouse established for the relief maintenance and employment of the Poor on the twenty second day of november instant at the Parish of Saint Mary in Stafford in the said County did refuse to work at work suited to his Age strength and capacity, to wit, Oakum Picking contrary to the form of the statute in that case made and provided And I the said Justice do Adjudge, that the said John Brown shall for the said Offence be imprisoned in the House of Correction at Stafford in and for the said County and there kept to hard Labour without Bail or Mainprize for the space of twenty one days*

Given under *my* hand and seal the day and year first above-

Punishments were set out in the commissioners' rules.

WORKHOUSE (Rules of Conduct)

Any Pauper who shall neglect to observe such of the regulations herein contained as are applicable to and binding on him: –

Or who shall make any noise when silence is ordered to be kept;
Or shall use obscene or profane language;
Or shall refuse or neglect to work, after having been required to do so;
Or shall play at cards or other games of chance;

Shall be deemed DISORDERLY.

Any pauper who shall within seven days, repeat any one or commit more than one of the offences specified . . .
Or shall by word or deed insult or revile the master or matron, or any other officer of the workhouse, or any of the Guardians;
Or shall be drunk;
Or shall wilfully disturb the other inmates during prayers or divine worship

Shall be deemed REFRACTORY

It shall be lawful for the master of the workhouse . . . to punish any disorderly *pauper by substituting, during a time not greater than forty-eight hours, for his or her dinner, as prescribed by the dietary, a meal consisting of eight ounces of bread, or one pound of cooked potatoes and also by witholding from him during the same period, all butter, cheese, tea, sugar, or broth . . .*

And it shall be lawful for the Board of Guardians . . . to order any refractory *pauper to be punished by confinement to a separate room, with or without an alteration of the diet . . . for . . . (no longer than) twenty-four hours . . .*

Rules drawn up by the commissioners in their Seventh Annual Report, 1841

Questions

1 Look again at the classification of paupers on page 43, and the Rules of Conduct on pages 44–5. Now read the following statements and say whether or not they are correct:
   a) The rules for the workhouse applied to everyone in the workhouse at any time.
   b) The only paupers who were allowed to meet members of their families were able-bodied married couples.
   c) Paupers who were ill, and children, did not have to follow the strict rules which set out the times of their working day.

2 The illustration by Cruickshank (page 46) shows Oliver Twist asking for more food. The Stafford Dietary (page 46) sets out

the food given to able-bodied paupers in Stafford workhouse at about the same time as Charles Dickens wrote *Oliver Twist.*

The Dietary suggests that the paupers had a lot of food. Does this mean that Charles Dickens was quite wrong to make Oliver 'ask for more'? Explain your answer very carefully – and think about it first!

3   The document on page 47 shows how a pauper was punished for refusing to work.
   a)   What had John Brown refused to do?
   b)   What was his punishment?
   c)   Look at the workhouse rules of conduct (page 48). What punishment was given for paupers who refused to work?
       John Brown's punishment was harsher than this. Can you make any suggestions as to why that was so?

This illustration, showing a poor family asking to be admitted to a workhouse, is from Jessie Phillips, *a novel written by Mrs Trollope in 1844 as a criticism of the New Poor Law*

It was not so much the living conditions which made paupers hate and fear the workhouse; it was the fact that an inmate lost his or her self-respect and identity. As we have seen, each pauper had to wear a uniform and lived a life that was regulated down to the last minute, separated from other members of their family.

The opposition to the New Poor Law

The New Poor Law was first introduced into the industrial midlands and north in 1837. Outdoor relief was vital for industrial workers in the north at those times when trade was slack and they were out of work until it picked up again. It was unfortunate that at this time there was a slump in the textile trade and there were large numbers of unemployed workers who were in great need of outdoor relief. The assistant commissioner, Alfred Power, whose job it was to introduce the new regulations into the West Riding of Yorkshire, was much disliked for his rigid personality. He was just not the sort of person to persuade people that it was all in their best interests.

It was not only the poor and the unemployed who opposed the new system in the northern industrial areas. In Huddersfield, opposition was led by Richard Oastler, a local woollen manufacturer. He toured the country trying to stir up opposition:

What is the principle of the New Poor Law? The condition imposed by Englishmen by that accursed law is, that man shall give up his liberty to save his life! That, before he shall eat a piece of bread, he shall go into prison . . .
Richard Oastler: *The Right of the Poor to Liberty and Life,* 1838

John Fielden, a factory owner from Todmorden, not far from Huddersfield, was also a Member of Parliament, and he led a successful campaign against the introduction of the Poor Law into Todmorden. When Fielden and others refused to pay the poor rate, two constables were sent to seize goods to pay the fine:

> *From all sides hundreds of angry men and women hurried to the village. A terrible scene ensued. The horse and cart were thrown violently down, with one of the constables on top. The cart was smashed and burned. The two constables were compelled by the mob to swear never to engage in the like business again.*
>
> Joshua Holden: *A Short History of Todmorden*, 1912

compelled: forced

It was not until 1877, a long time after Fielden's death, that Todmorden at last agreed to build its own workhouse.

In Bradford, the Guardians of the Poor and the assistant commissioner, Alfred Power, were threatened by the mob. Mr Power was pelted with stones and tin cans! At another meeting, soldiers had to be called in to break up the rioting crowd.

Local people (and not just paupers) made attacks on workhouses. The picture below is an artist's impression of the attack on Stockport workhouse in 1842.

From The Illustrated London News, *1842*

1 a) For what reasons did the people riot in both Todmorden
       and Stockport?
   b) How do the illustration on page 49 and the extract from
       Richard Oastler's book (page 49) help to show why people
       attacked workhouses?

2 The picture of the attack on Stockport workhouse shows people
   who were reasonably well-dressed, and who were, we may
   presume, not paupers. Why might better-off people have joined
   in attacks on workhouses?

The Poor Law Commission was forced to allow outdoor relief for the able-bodied poor in many areas of the north. The difficulties here led the commission to issue, in 1842, an order which became known as the 'Labour Test'. This laid down that where there were more male, able-bodied paupers than the workhouse could contain, these men should be 'tested' by being given work to do. Those who could cope with the work would not be admitted to the workhouse, and could claim outdoor relief.

In the south the picture was different. By 1841, the commission had given orders to about four-fifths of the unions, forbidding outdoor relief to the adult able-bodied poor. In 1842, these orders were given to rural unions in the north, and in 1844 a General Order was issued, which was to replace all the individual orders. This general order prohibited outdoor relief for all able-bodied paupers and their families, with the exception of the sick, widows with children, and those who had recently been widowed. Another clause of the order allowed paupers to claim outdoor relief 'where such person shall require relief on account of sudden and urgent necessity'. This could always be used as a reason for giving outdoor relief, for the commission had not said anything about what they considered to be 'urgent necessity'. It would be up to the individual Boards of Guardians to decide on each case.

What this meant was that outdoor relief was never completely abolished, even in the south. By 1847, the Poor Law Board, which replaced the commission in that year, had given up hope of prohibiting outdoor relief in 142 of the unions – one fifth of the total number. Outdoor relief must have continued in many other unions, when paupers were able to convince the guardians that they came under the headings in the 1844 General Order which allowed outdoor relief.

Why was there so much opposition in the north? It seems that the people were worried on two main counts. Their first fear was that the commissioners were going to ignore the special problems arising from periodic unemployment in northern industrial towns. They feared the commissioners were going to impose upon them the same regulations for dealing with the poor as those which they had heard had been introduced in the south. As you have seen in this chapter, the rules to be followed by the guardians were not the same in every union; local differences *were* noted. This did not prevent rumours that every pauper was going to be forced into the workhouse. In Bradford, for example, they were not used to the idea of large numbers of people having to go into the workhouse. Between 1812 and 1815, only 157 out of an annual average of 1 605 paupers had been admitted to the old poorhouse. The rest had received outdoor relief.

Their second fear was one which every area of the country shared: they were very suspicious of regulations which came from London. The Old Poor Law had become very much a matter for the local communities, and people were worried that the commission in London would dominate the local Boards of Guardians. There were also rumours of dreadful workhouse conditions. The cartoon below shows what people believed to be some of the differences between the Old and the New Poor Law.

What do you think the cartoonist's attitude is to the Old Poor Law and to the New Poor Law?

On the whole, much was achieved in the first ten years or so of the New Poor Law. It was not always what the commissioners who compiled the report had wanted; it was not usually, if ever, welcomed by the paupers themselves. It did, however, help to bring down the poor rate, and many people were pleased with what they saw being done in the Poor Law unions.

Using the evidence

A   This Bradford broadsheet probably dates from the years just after the introduction of the New Poor Law:

The New Starvation Law examined,
And some Description of the Food, Dress, Labour and Regulations, imposed upon the poor and unfortunate sufferers in the New British Bastiles.

Come you men and women unto me attend,
And listen and see what for you I have penn'd;
And if you do buy it, and carefully read,
T'will make your hearts within you to bleed.

The lions at London, with their cruel paw,
You know they have pass'd a Starvation Law;
These tigers and wolves should be chained in a den,
Without power to worry poor women and men.

When a man and his wife for sixty long years
Have toiled together through troubles and fears,
And brought up a family with prudence and care,
To be sent to the Bastile it's very unfair.

And in the Bastile each woman and man
Is parted asunder, – is this a good plan?
A word of sweet comfort they cannot express,
For unto each other they ne'er have access.

To give them hard labour, it is understood.
In handmills the grain they must grind for their feed,
Like men in a prison they work them in gangs,
With turning and twisting it fills them with pangs.

I'll give you an insight of their regulations,
Which they put in force in these situations,
They've school, chapel, and prison all under a roof,
And the governor's house stands a little aloof.

The master instructs them the law to obey,
The governor minds it's all work and no play,
And as for religion the parson doth teach
That he knows the gospel, – no other must preach.

Ye hard-working men, wherever you be,
I'd have you watch closely these men, d'ye see;
I think they're contriving, the country all o'er,
To see what's the worst they can do to the poor.

B   These two illustrations are from *Jessie Phillips*, a novel
published in 1844.

A women's ward: cripples, old women and the
mentally ill all lived together

A meeting of the Board of Guardians. The
guardians have been so harsh that a woman
asking for relief has fainted

C   *Plain as is the fare, it was better than the old man had existed
on for years; but though better it was not his dinner. He was
not sitting in his old chair, at his old table, round which his
children once gathered. He had not planted the cabbage,
and tended it while it grew, and cut it himself. At home he
could lift the latch of the garden gate and go down the road if
he wished. Here he could not go outside the boundary – it
was against the regulations.*

R. Jefferies: *Hodge and his Masters*, 1880

D   *The positive good which has been wrought by the new Poor
Law is, in the first place, that the public houses and beer
shops are, without question, much less attended than
before: that drunkenness is decidedly less frequently seen,
and I think practised.*

From the Second Annual Report of the Poor Law Commissioners,
1836. Evidence given by the Rev. Dr Wrench, Minister of Salehurst

E *At a meeting of the Board of Guardians held at Highworth, on Wednesday the 11th of January, 1837, the following Resolutions were moved, seconded, and carried unanimously:*

That the Board regard with satisfaction the working of the Poor Law Amendment Act, during the twelve months it has been in operation in this Union of sixteen parishes, and 12,611 population.

That the financial savings of the ratepayers, since the formation of the Union, as compared with the average expenditure of the three preceeding years, is upwards of 54 per cent per annum. . . . This financial saving is also attended with decided symptoms of returning industry among the labouring poor, and it is evident that the new law is working a great moral improvement in the habits of this class of people.

From the Third Annual Report of the Poor Law
Commisioners, 1837

1   Make a list of all the criticisms of workhouses which you can find in the broadsheet (source **A**) and in the illustrations (source **B**).

2   Look again at the list which you made for Question 1. Broadsheets were one of the few ways in which the poor could broadcast their feelings. The illustrations come from a book which was written specifically against the New Poor Law. Does this mean that we cannot use these sources (**A** and **B**) as evidence of how people felt about the New Poor Law?

3   How does source **C** help to show why the poor objected to workhouses?

4   Not everyone was against the New Poor Law. The people who reported to the commissioners (sources **D** and **E**) certainly approved of the effects of the new arrangements.
    Explain why Dr Wrench and the Highworth Guardians approved of the New Poor Law. Do you think that these results were what the commissioners had in mind when they wrote their report?

INDEX